Etching “The Kitchen” by James McNeil Whistler

Carol E. R. Doering

Touch of Remembrance

Remembrance, a touch of yesterday, no matter how long ago. A walk in the quiet forest on a path lined with violets, the smell of a favorite meal cooking, or a familiar hug by a special person. Let me take you down that path with all of its remembrances. Travel the way of ocean sounds, tree leaves moving to the wind's rhythm, the silence of your kitchen at dawn, laughter of a small child. Come with me along the path of remembrance.

Carol E. R. Doering

ACKNOWLEGEMENTS

Cover by: Eleanor Knight, Watercolorist, Fergus, Ontario, Canada. This is the third cover that Eleanor has painted for me. It is amazing, that all I have to do is give her a title and she works the miracle. This is a cover that entices the reader to open the book to see the remembrances written inside.

Etchings: James McNeil Whistler, Book #32 dated 1932 – "The Kitchen" 1858 Etching Plate I. James McBey, Book #2 dated 1924 – "Gamrie" Etching Plate VI.
The poem "My Time" was published in an anthology "Walk Through Paradise" 1995, ISBN 1-56167-285-8
All rights remained with the author.
Photographs by the author, C. Doering

FIRST EDITION

Library of Congress Catalog Number – Pending
ISBN: 0-9652754-3-4
Printed in the United States of America
R.A.D. Works, 2746 Tennyson Street
Thousand Oaks, Ca 91360-1630

DEDICATION

Being dedicated to writing, no matter the form, can become a secondary part of one's life. Involvement in many other things can distract from creativity.

When the wall became too high around me, blocking all avenues of writing, my fellow Pen Women, Frances Riley, Diantha Ain and Robin Westmiller helped to break down the barriers and gave me encouragement to go forth.

Eleanor Knight, my Canadian friend and watercolorist was inspired again and the painting she did for this book cover conveys the title "Touch of Remembrance" with soft colors and a timely subject.

To my husband, Richard and daughter Sally Anne, thanks for giving me the time to write.

And without my faith in the one who guides me, no words/poetry would be possible.

INDEX

INDEX

SIT BESIDE ME AND
HEAR MY WORDS

Sit beside me and hear my words
Open your heart and gather them in
The words are feelings that flow through you
like water rushing down a turbulent stream

Sit down beside me and hear the story ring true
Reach out and touch it, see it, feel it
Watch the colors flow through the words
Paint your own pictures as they glide across your mind

Sit down at my feet
Feel the waves of emotion breaking over you with each new verse
Grab it with your mind, taste it on your tongue,
savor the flavor until it envelopes your whole being

Come sit down beside me, hear and enjoy the words spoken by the teller

NATURE'S MAJESTY

NATURE'S MAJESTY

On the edge of time, clouds, sun and ocean clash
Lightning flashes overhead amidst dark clouds
Sun peers through a break in the darkness
reaching to spread its last rays upon the calm
ocean
The bright reflection of light dances along tips of
low waves racing to beat the darkness
The sun slips off the edge of the earth and night
descends

MY TIME

Listen and you can hear the silence
The time when daylight intrudes upon the night
You can see the dew on the grass and the snails hurrying home before the sun makes the ground too warm
The birds have already begun their chirping and fly to catch the night bugs rushing homeward
The silence is soothing allowing the mind and body to be at peace
This is my time, before the night is gone and the sun rises
The time when everyone is asleep, when I can sit and think about days gone by or just sit listening to the silence
It is my time to make my peace with God and myself.
To me this is the most beautiful time of day, when the noise is subdued and the shine of the early light is not on the horizon
This is my time and I thank the Lord for the peace and silence, so I may renew myself for the hustle and activity of the world

PORCELAIN PETALS

PORCELAIN PETALS

The morning mist hangs low over the valley
Droplets of clear moisture cling to every branch and leaf
Only the sound of water slipping to earth is heard
Nestled close to tree roots, the snow white, delicate porcelain petals of the orchid cling to slender green stems
Each flower gleams as if touched by the purity of angels wings
They lift their heads, and pray for just one touch of warmth from the filtered sun
No sweet smell wafts upward, but I want to bend down and cup each flower in my hand so I can see and touch the velvety petals

INDIAN MAIDEN

Wandering through the art gallery, splashes of
vivid color catch the eye
Paintings of native people abound, some harsh,
some dramatic
These are the people of Alaska
One small painting, done on a brown paper bag,
beckons to all
When standing before it, the Indian Maiden sends
a message to the onlooker
Holding her head high, she portrays her proud
heritage
The brown paper background gives the painting
an added glow as if invisible sunlight shines
behind it
Skin is clear and mocha-colored
Cheeks rosy from the cold glacier air
Eyes deep brown with a softness that begs the
viewer to know her
She appears to reach out, with the warmth of
friendship drawing the viewer closer, tempting
them
Hair is pulled straight back with small strands
stroking the sides of her face
Colored feathers are all that adorn black hair and
a doeskin dress is brightly decorated with beads
and stitching
Gazing at the Indian Maiden, I look for more and
am unable to turn away
The artist must have loved her so dearly, to put
his love on canvas, keeping her image with him
always

SAPPHIRE DRAGON TREE

SAPPHIRE DRAGON TREE

SAPPHIRE DRAGON TREE

Climbing the winding pathway through the garden
of blossoms
Rounding a bend, a profusion of purple blocks
the view of the sky
A sapphire dragon tree spreads itself, extending
upward
Walking beneath the giant flowers, a shower of
purple rains down upon me
Gathering the buds and crushing them, sweet
smells of dragon tree burst forth
A vision of purple satin and the scent of finest
perfumes surround as you stand beneath its
beauty
The wind gently blows, again releasing purple
sapphires

NATURE'S WRATH

Anger swells the rushing sea
Winds sweep across crests of foaming waves
Rocky barriers stand guard trying to protect the beach
Closer and higher the waves advance, daring anyone to get in their way
Pounding, pounding the sound of thunder from the sea
Waves, a giant water monster threatening the beach
Rain beats down without mercy, rivers rise flowing to the sea as if in deaths' final throes
Soon the sea wins out rolling over the land and moves inward, retreating, only to come again more violently
Mindless destruction, but soon nature's wrath senses it has done maximum damage and it retreats back across the shore
Peace comes again to the ocean
The waves gently touch the shore and calmness prevails

CLEOPATRA'S CHILD

CLEOPATRA'S CHILD

She enters the room, and we are sent back in time
Head held high, hair braided, framing her face
Skin the color of coffee with just a drop of cream
Eyes that shine like polished ebony
Slim and graceful she moves with the elegance of a young gazelle, proud of who she is today
Her features are chiseled from a classic mold but blended with softness
The beauty of Cleopatra with the carriage of a modern girl
A child, teenager, and soon to be a woman who will always wear the face of ancient days

I'M NEAR

Can you feel it in the wind as it brushes your
mind, it is me, I'm here
As you stand at the edge of the ocean, each
ripple striking the shore, making soothing sounds,
I'm there
My touch comes to you when stress overwhelms
The light kiss on your cheek is me, I am always
by your side
We are soul mates, mother and daughter
When you look in the mirror, a piece of me
reflects back
As you are working and a child asks a question
your answer is part of me
I will miss your loving care, always putting me first
I have moved from your mortal realm to a place of
peace and tranquility
But near you I will forever be
Love does not die only the shell we use as
mortals
Love stays forever, and you pass it on, never
letting it fade

MORNING GLORY

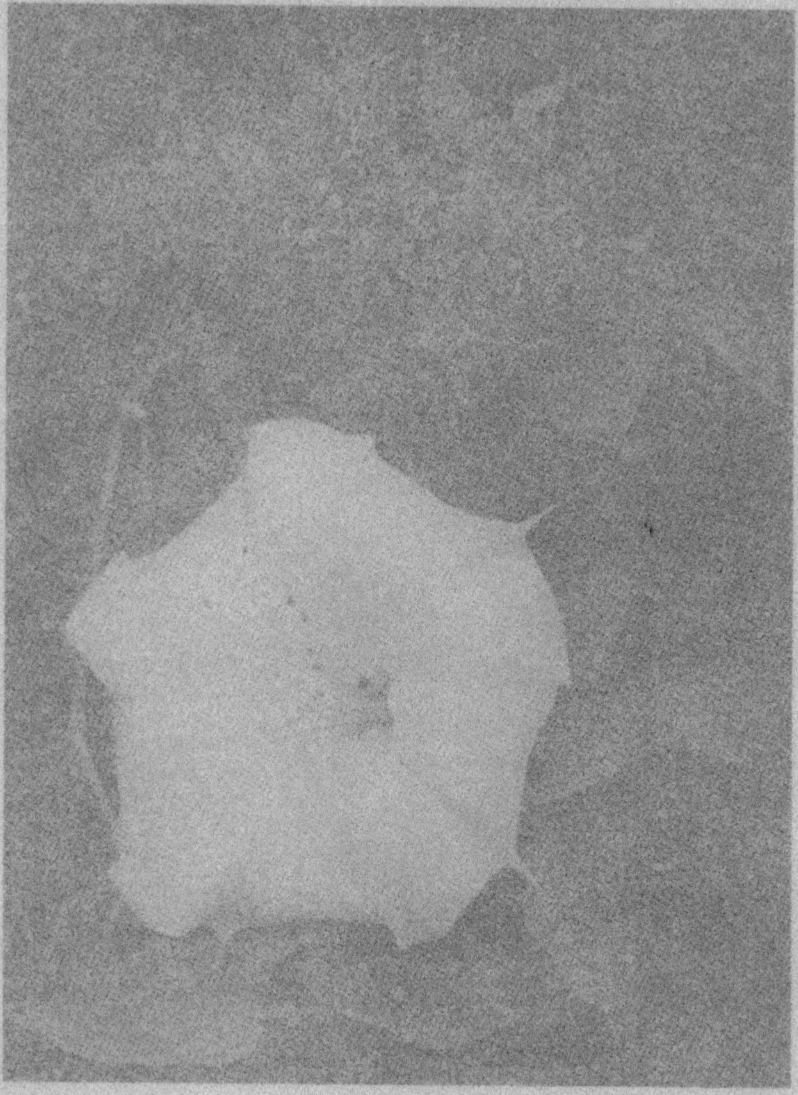

MORNING GLORY

MORNING GLORY

Brambles, cactus, leaves drying and a sturdy vine
winds it's way along the embankment, sprouting
white blossoms with darkened edges
In the early morning, moisture beads across
purple tinged petals, and ants rush to gather the
nectar deep within its center
Delicate lavender pistils sway as each small body
brushes by them
When morning recedes, the worker-ants retreat
as the flower closes, resting until the morrow

MIRROR FRIENDS

We moved from familiar places to the unknown
My life at five became an empty shell, my
playmates miles away
One day when all hope was lost to my young
mind, my mother sensing my despair, took me by
the hand and lead me to her special mirror
We stood side by side, gazing at the strangers
"Hello Mary she said, did you want a friend"
"Hello Helen can I tell you my sad story"
My mother had given me not one friend but two
The years have passed but still we stand before
the mirror, mother, her friend, daughter, her friend
and the loneliness that existed at five
We stand to tell the truth at last to each other,
that without the compassion given by my mother,
the daughter might not have grown to be
someone's friend
Friends, whether imaginary, real or a part of
ourselves are the basis by which we live
My mirror friends will always be a part of me

YOU DON'T KNOW ME

YOU DON'T KNOW ME

Before you destroyed our buildings, did you learn about me?
Before you killed us did you ask if we hate you?
You don't know me
Did you read our history to know what we are all about
You blew up our buildings, you destroyed people from many countries but you failed to destroy our country
You don't know me
Our history reveals a country united and proud
On a ship in the harbor many years ago, a captain asked one simple questions, "Does 'it' still fly?"
The answer came loud and clear, "Yes our flag still stands"
On a hill in the South Pacific, the flag was raised high and it still does wave
The Arizona remains our standard bearer, the flag still flies above it
You don't know me
On a street in New York City the rubble was piled high but the flag of our nation remained unscathed bearing its proud colors above the smoke and dust
You don't know me, or my people
The harder you try, the tougher we get
You don't know me and until you do no matter how hard you try to destroy me, you will find a sleeping giant awakened
You don't know me

CREATIVE SELF

The fire blazes brightly upon the hearth
Spikes of yellow, red and white shoot upward
Heat and smoke rushing up the chimney
It is night, and I sit in front of the fireplace
Quietness surrounds me, and my creative self is at rest
The cares of the day have been shut out, and the night forms a soft blanket of darkness
Sleeps pushes at the edge of my mind
A log drops startling me into wakefulness
I realize that today is the accumulation of all my yesterdays
Thoughts slowly drift into emptiness
Finally sleeps claims my body and all is at rest

STICK BIRDS

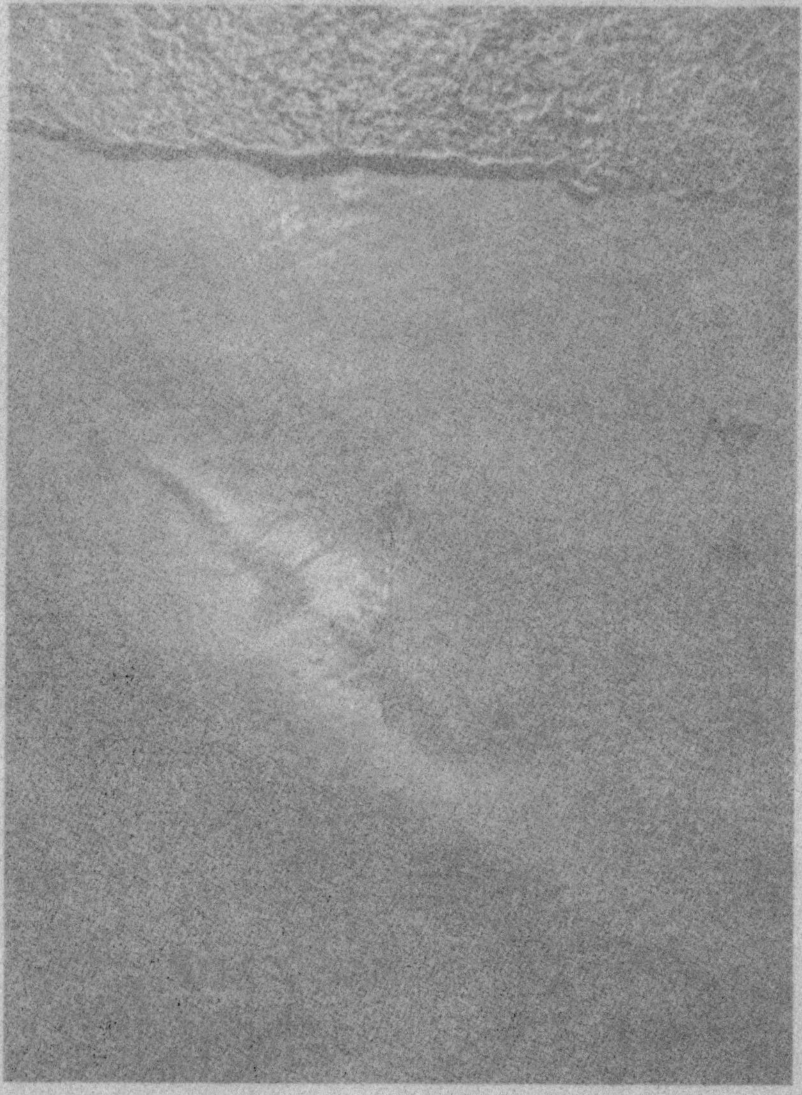

STICK BIRDS

Surf beating towards shore
Surfers riding the waves that flatten on the
shoreline
Hurrying to meet the surf's foam, stick birds race
to the water
Long beaks probing the sand for unsuspecting
crabs
Gray and white speckled birds with tall legs
moving to beat the returning waves
Tiny blue gray, racing birds see the water arriving,
rush to shore, not wanting to get their feet wet
The sea, and the stick birds imitating the waves,
one of natures ultimate consistencies

SILENCE

A raindrop falls in the forest and is never heard
Rushing footsteps in a hospital ward, with no sound of footfall made
The wind rushes through the treetops, and the sounds we hear are trees brushing one against another, not the wind
We sit in church and pray, the silence surrounds us
In the early morning when sleep evades and no one else is up, sitting and listening to the silence, making peace with time
On a dark night looking towards the east, the full moon bursts forth silently lighting up the blackened sky
Silence, the healer of hurts, it speaks a thousand words but says nothing
Silence, the never-ending tide that fills the voids and canyons of the mind, giving peace to troubled souls
Silence, a state of mind at rest

WINTER DIAMONDS

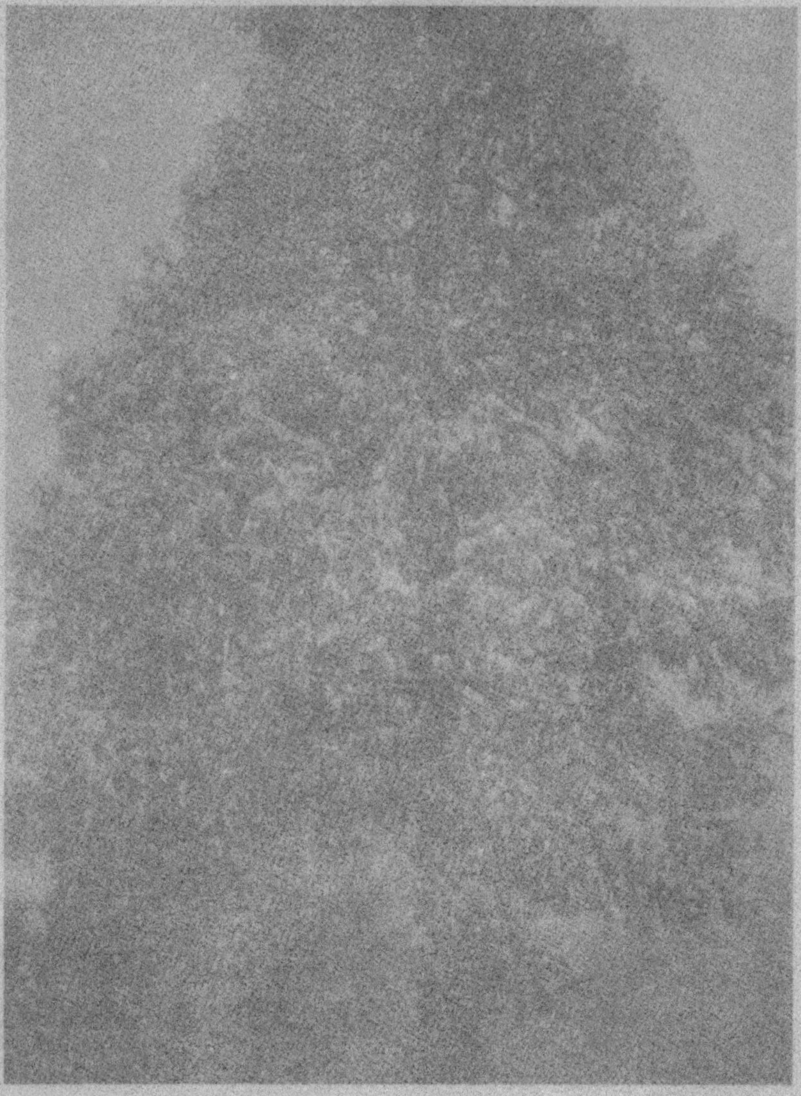

WINTER DIAMONDS

Sleep retreats as morning comes and to our
surprise, we awaken to a world of snow,
whiteness covering every space
Man has not blemished the purity, but God's
creatures have made their mark
Small footprints dot the smooth covered
pathways
Tiny bird tracks, arrows pointing in every direction
Three-toed deer prints make a path like sentries
on watch
Coyotes howling for joy in the early morning hour
The sun finally breaks through, and our world is
turned into sparkling diamonds
Pine tree branches glisten from melting snow
And each little breeze brings snow tumbling from
the branches overhead
The sun does not stay, but the sparkling
memories remain

TEA PARTY

She arrives all in lace from her hat to the tips of her fingers
The sweep of her long dress accents her late entrance, and her fancy hat shades this slim mortal from all who watch
The tables are covered with cloths of linen and the cups are the finest china
Arranged on the delicate platter, pink and white cakes
She is seated at a small, round table, a vision of lace joins the guests
Her tea is poured from a flowered pot, not a drop is spilled
Her conversation falls on deaf ears and no one replies
Miss Tabby and Misty, the cats, and Max the dog can only meow and bark
Her mother calls from the back porch, time for a nap
The tea party is ended
The illusions remain and in the future, she will attend a very real tea party, all dressed up in lace

MR. ABALONE

MR. ABALONE

MR. ABALONE

On a clear, sunny, winter day I stroll along the sandy beach
Tide has moved the water out beyond reach
No rocks mar this place, seashells arrive in one piece
Small pools of water gather at low spots in the sand
I come upon this knobby cone-shaped shell, barnacles decorate it
Curious, I pick it up only to find it has a resident
Gently I poke its soft underside and it curls back into the shell
The inside of its home is rainbow-colored and I know I have met, Mr. Abalone
He has been swept out of the sea, beached high and almost dry
Should I take him home, no he will surely die
I find a deep spot where the tide is returning and give him back to the sea

SHADOWS UPON HER FACE

She peers through the raindrops, which make trails on the window panes
God's tears reflect shadows on her lovely face
Her head rests on folded hands, never moving, seeing only the wet world outside the window
The tree branches gently move against the house, scattering moisture
Peace and quiet are etched upon her face because the outside world remains at bay
Her stillness reaches out and tells us to be at peace
The sun breaks through, and a glow pushes away the shadows on her lovely face

COLORED REFLECTIONS

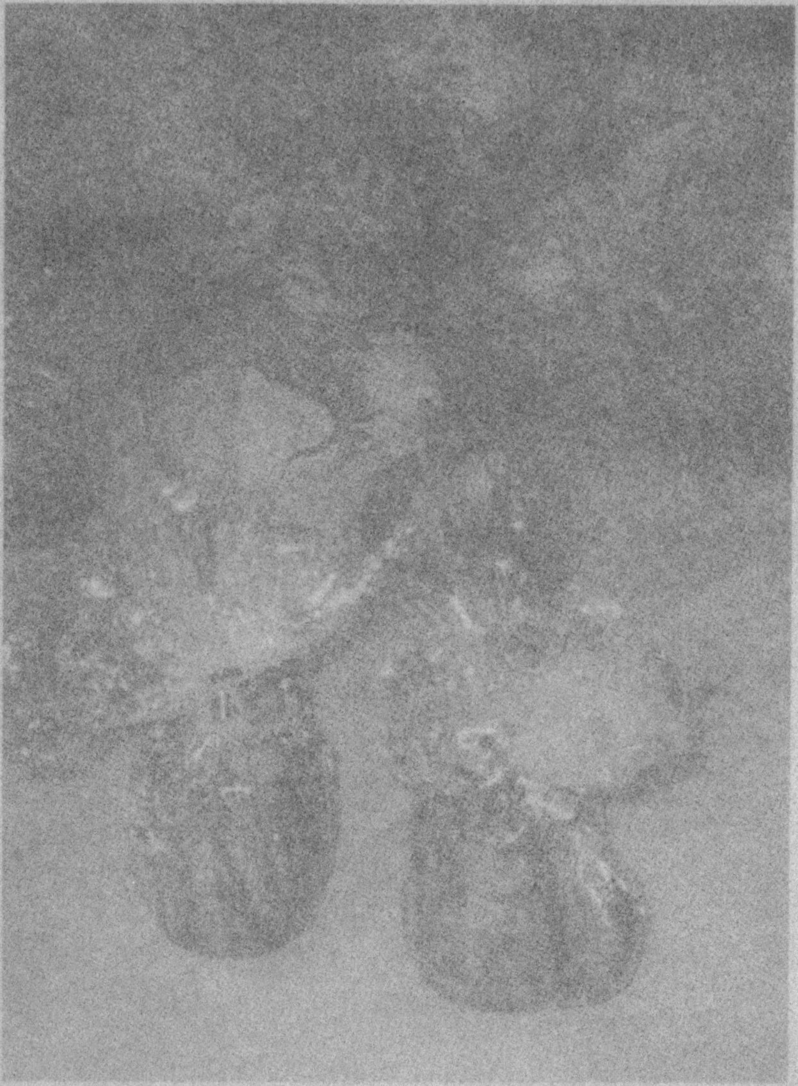

COLORED REFLECTIONS

In the center of the table, flowers of every hue
contrast against pure white of the cloth
Translucent paper on gifts spread its colors like
bright reflecting lights
Illumination coming from above pierces through
the paper making symmetrically shaped rainbows
Tangled ribbon, leaves of different shapes and
sharp pointed images in lavender, blues, greens
and yellows change white cloth into an artist
palette
The artistic pleasure of light filtered through
colored paper

PLACE OF PEACE

When days are turbulent I long for a place of peace
The window of stained glass angels overlook the windblown, but quiet place
In springtime when all the leaves burst forth, orange and cherry blossoms wait to share their sweet scent
Clusters of purple-blue flowers are covered with yellow bees tasting the sweet nectar of each bloom
Smell the newly turned moist soil and see bulbs pushing their green heads upwards, peeking to see the sun
Lizards rush across the cool walkway, scurrying from one shelter to the next
The peace of this spot gently touches my innermost self
I have found my peaceful place and the turbulence is at rest

BEACH SQUIRREL

BEACH SQUIRREL

BEACH SQUIRREL

A high pitched whistle floats across the shoreline
Danger, danger watch out people are here
He stands on his hind legs, tail at attention
guarding his territory
Nose twitching to catch the foreign scent of man
More sentries arrive, brown and speckled, tails
waving to ward off the danger
Throw a few morsels of bread, chips and cheese
Quickly they scramble to snatch it, retreating to
the crevices in the rocky shore
Sentry squirrels marking their ever-changing
territory

MISSING YOU

My life, days and nights seem never ending
Loneliness covers my mind like a shroud and a darkness descends
I sit by the window, my opening to the world
Looking out, I always expect some pain, some joy and some ending
I wait for someone to come who will tell me truly that at day's end I'll be with you
But still from morning sun to the first night shadows I look for known shapes and listen for familiar voices
In your peaceful resting place, will you watch over me, and know that I will always be waiting for the time of togetherness

COLOR ME AUTUMN

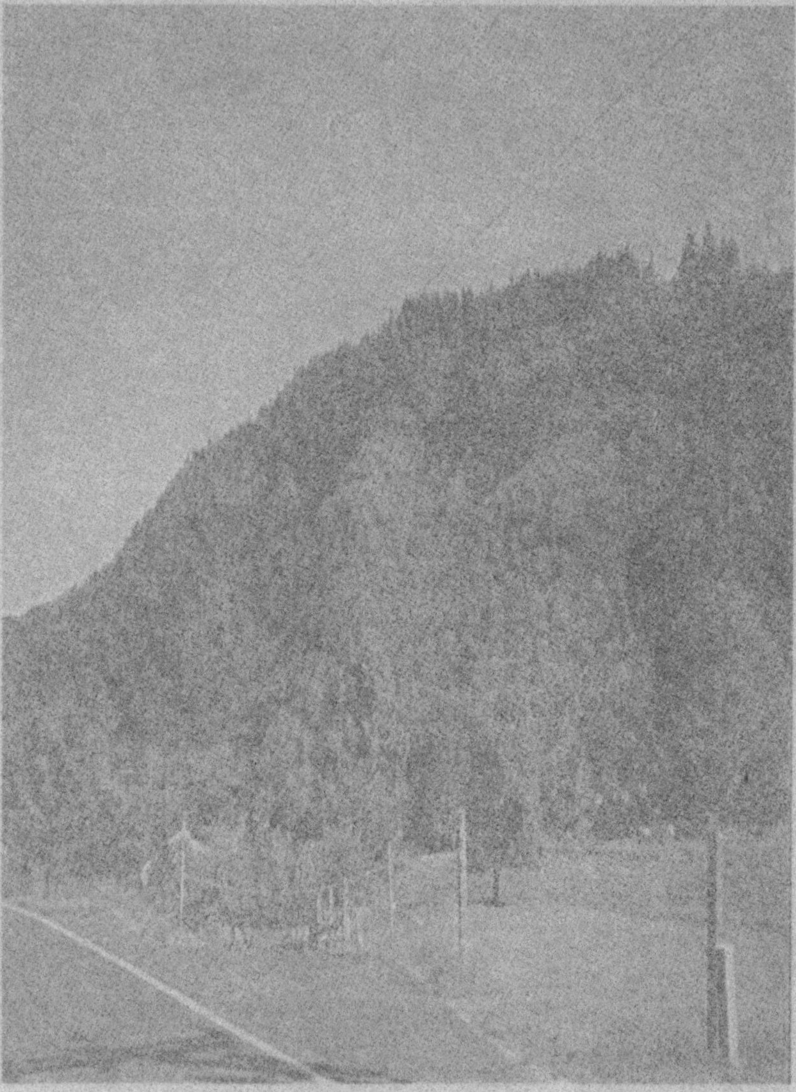

COLOR ME AUTUMN

Country road tunneled by trees blocking out the light
Houses peak through dense greenery
Soon the forest, which surrounds us, opens into stark grassy fields and pastures
Sunlight bursts forth bathing everything in sight
High on the mountain top, the evergreen trees dominate the hillsides
But like an artist whose brush has gone wild, in the darkness of green, splashes of color burst forth
A sea of reds and oranges, gently touched by the warm breeze, sway amidst the towering giants

GREAT WHITE OWL

The silence of the night is broken by the soft,
hooting of the great white owl
The sound travels through the cold waves of night
air, each call different than the last
He perches upon the snow-covered branches,
hidden from view, becoming part of the winter
scene
I stand in the frosty night air watching and
listening, awaiting his next flight
All at once snow tumbles from the branches and
he takes flight, massive white wings lifting him up
to the jet-black sky
Does he hunt for prey or is his flight just for the
joy of soaring into the dark night?
The sound of beating wings retreat as he climbs
higher
He is as a falling star streaking across the
heavens, one-minute white lightning, the next
darkness

JAPANESE BLOSSOMS

JAPANESE BLOSSOMS

JAPANESE BLOSSOMS

Towering over the crowds of Japanese cherry
trees, the Washington Monument rises high
above the park
The sky is blotted out by cascading branches of
flowers
Blush pink and angel white, the blossoms rain
down upon our heads as we walk down green
paths
There is no overwhelming fragrance, just the
beauty of flowers covering the park with clouds of
pale colors
Nature's wonder, gone in the blink of an eye but
which is etched in our memories

MEMORIES

When the birds sing in the meadow
And the flowers drop their petals
When the wind whispers through the trees
And the raindrops tap on your windows
Remember me as I was, not as I had become
So many memories to fall back upon
I'm there for you as you were for me
Remember the little boy who held your hand
The first steps I took and the first ball I threw
Remember my first Christmas, and when I first drove the car too
Reach out with your heart and mind, I'm there
Not forgotten, not stored in a memory box but always within you and always with love

FURRY ELEPHANT

FURRY ELEPHANT

I think an elephant lives in our house
She's the funniest looking elephant, all furry and soft
No trumpet noise does she make but meow, meow
I think an elephant lives in my house
In the quiet of the day, a great thundering noise sounds overhead
I know it must be elephants, but as I peak around the stairwell, bright blue eyes gaze down at me
No elephant do I see but a ball of fluff named Misty

SHADOWS OF THE NIGHT

We sit around the fire on a small spit of sand,
thinking of ways to renew our youth
And as in our youth, we will stay up for the
coming of the dawn
A tow headed child and her father come out of
the darkness to share and warm themselves by
the fire
They appeared like night shadows, ragged in
appearance but comfortable around us
We tell our stories and sing into the night.
Music played by the father resounds across the
water, adding fullness to our song
In the stillness of the night before the darkness
meets the light they disappear
The laughter of the child, the deep tones of the
father drift back across the sand and then are
gone
Like shadows of the night they vanish in the rising
sunlight.

WINTER WILLOW

WINTER WILLOW

In summer leaves of sweeping green hide my graying trunk
My branches protect the small birds and dragon flies
Winter comes and all is revealed
Crusty trunk, knurled limbs and bare branches
A different beauty, all gray with a tinge of green
Branches waiting for the spring to let me burst into bloom
The lake still laps at my base and ducks remain nestled at my roots
Dried leaves have settled in the top of my trunk keeping warm the stem of life within waiting for a new season

DEER IN THE MIST

The morning hours come quickly
Fog covers the mountains, touching brown hills
I walk in the morning mist surrounded by the
silence
A family of deer graze on the shrouded hillside
They move about always vigilant for predators
A coyote howls in the hills high above and the
deer scatter, startled by the wild presence
The fog covers all again and silence returns

STEPS OF WATER

STEPS OF WATER

Can you hear it?
The gentle flow of water moving across steps of granite
High on the hill it flows clear as glass making its own music as it travels downward
Sunlight casts its reflection upon moving water flowing into small pools
Plunging into a final well, spouting up, sharing its gift of soothing sounds
Then it starts the journey again

A GAME OF CLOUDS

Each morning we begin our journey anew
We travel closer to snow-covered mountains,
layered with heavy clouds
Wispy bits of white fluff drop from on high, playing
leapfrog into the valleys
The small puffs touch the earth and spring
skyward like children on a trampoline
The billowing bouncers seem to use the wind as a
springboard, frolicking high to the mountain top
then sweeping low again
The wind drops into the valley and the mountain
is covered with clouds again
Time called, game ended until the wind calls the
clouds again

THE PLACE

THE PLACE

The laughter of small children, the caw of many
large crows, and also the silence of a special
place
Peace that is worn like a comfortable warm cloak
Tall trees reach skyward from a small island, a
sanctuary filled with feathered wildlife
High in the tree tops the leaves and branches
give the appearance of white clouds
Snow white egrets perch upon slender branches
The geese strut in formation chasing anyone in
their path
Soon they enter the stream, floating like Venetian
warships, gliding to the island
They declare their rule of the water by honking
The squirrels chase one another from tree to tree,
pouncing on each other playfully
Sunlight filters through the trees, touching here
and there
Silence gathers around the bench, and peaceful
solitude covers the park, and all who observe
nature's wonders

LONELINESS

It moves like a cloud with no end, blanketing my
mind and body
Loneliness gives me no quarter, attacking at my
most unprotected times
When it arrives the will to do or say anything is
set aside
I just want to hide
Loneliness spreading its residue feelings,
clouding the mind, and the taste with bitterness
Shaking myself back to reality, I know it will return
It is not a resident, only an unwelcome guest
If only I could change the shape of loneliness and
see beyond the emptiness, maybe the next time it
arrives I could step aside.

WATCH DOG

WATCH DOG

We have this here dog, looks like a bear, eats like a bear
He's black and hairy, his feet are webbed, guess that means he can swim pretty good
Some people ask, "hey that your watch dog"
Yeah, he's mean and attacks
But what you really have to watch out for is his tongue, it must be two feet long
It always has slobber on it
We know when you entered our home in an unwelcome fashion
Your clothes covered with hair (don't wear white) and you'll be slimed from your head to your toes
Yeah, we have a watchdog but we'll never get sued, except maybe if you think we should pay for your cleaning bill

SUNFLOWER BONNET

The grocery store is busy as can be
I wait in line wondering why I always pick the one that has a problem
My temper rises and I'm about to leave the cart
But an elegant hat with a large sunflower appears
Looking beneath the bonnet I see the face of an angel
Tiny, but sweet and gentle
She, too, is impatient, her stroller is too confining
Her hat tilts sideways and covers one eye but the other lights up saying I'm going to escape when no one is watching
Impatience turns to giggles as she thinks about escape
How can anyone stay angry, when they see an angel, in a sunflower decorated bonnet

RINGS OF TIME

RINGS OF TIME

It must have been a giant of a tree
Reaching to the heavens and drinking in the
sunlight with every branch and leaf
Its rings of age, hidden beneath the heavy bark,
kept the secret of time
Recreation became its enemy, move tree we
need your space
The blade cuts deep, the sap ran freely and
God's gift no longer towers over all
Time and sun have changed all that remains
The stump is cracked, the bark dried out and
bleached white
The rings of age, still visible are disappearing, the
last stanza of the towering tree is being sung

GOODBYE

The years go, by but thoughts of goodbye stay
with me
Vietnam, a place of horror
The children racked by war, but wanting some
recognition
The wounded, whose eyes will forever linger in
my mind, haunt me
The destruction of the 'people's' property, with no
chance to rebuild
The hate of one people for another, each being of
the same nationality
Yet in spite of the pain, suffering of friend, foe,
and warrior, it was hard to say goodbye

JOURNEY

JOURNEY

To read of life just before the sun crests the
horizon is like awakening a giant light in one's
soul

To read of death when the last rays of sunlight
slip over the edge of the world is to realize that
life is limitless but it can disappear at the end of
each day

To experience life from first awakening to the
silence of the night is fulfillment on the journey
into the known and unknown

When the journey is ended and the world fades
we are complete and at peace

FRANCES

We wander the road of life in an off-handed way,
making friends and sometimes enemies
Many times God shines His special light on us
and then, we meet that one person who makes
our life more meaningful
Frances is my light at the end of a darkened
tunnel
Her shining glow, like a lightning bug, calms me
down and puts me on the path of reason
Helper, friend and always there when the need
arises
Be careful not to ask for too much or her fire will
turn to embers
Don't let her burn too brightly, we will then only
see sparks
Treat her as you would a favorite beloved antique
or a treasured memory to be kept for all times
Lent to me by Him, by His wondrous love, she is
God's special friend

THE BLUE TILED PAGODA

THE BLUE TILED PAGODA

The water rushes over large rocks, slipping under
the blue pagoda, drowning out worldly sounds
Koi swim in lazy circles in the calm pond making
ripples and rainbows on gentle waves
Tender young pines brush against large boulders,
bamboo stretches to gain the sun
Tiny lanterns light the way to quiet places under
the roof of the blue pagoda

SUZAN

She stands deep in the forest
Giant trees hide the filtering sun
Hands rising high trying to encompass God's handiwork
Hear her words fly outward reaching all who listen
Like the silence of the forest, which gathers the words to it, those who hear her grow in spirit, matching the strength of trees
When the words are gone, the teaching remains
God has given you a special gift
As angels dust every leaf and bloom, you touch the very soul of mankind

EARLY MORNING ON THE LAKE

EARLY MORNING
ON THE LAKE

Rising early to greet the first rays of daylight, I
gaze across the still waters
The lake is shrouded in steamy gray mist
The pure white herons break the surface, strutting
on long legs through the shadowed water
Bending down gracefully to catch the
unsuspecting water bugs
Signs of many fish cover the calm surface as they
come up for air, leaving bubbles on the water
Deer, ever cautious come to the water's edge
Orange and black dragonflies skim the lake
Turkey vultures patrol the shore, but when in flight
their wings cast dark shadows on the still water
Ducks swimming form triangles of displaced
water but when they dive pinwheels flowing
outward appear
The coyotes have been here, paw prints at the
water's edge declare their presence
Soon the full sun peeks over the mountain,
pushing the mist away
Once gray, then blue, and all at once a myriad of
colors deepen the lake's clear water
It has arrived, a new day

THE LONELY PINE

LONELY PINE

Along a lonely stretch of railroad track stands a Monterey pine
Branches blown north and east by strong ocean breezes
Squirrels, sea gulls and small creatures find safety amidst its flattened structure
Cactus march to overtake it but cannot cross the iron rails
Majestic in stature, lonely by nature, a solitary sentry on the barren beach front

TOMBOY

Meet the tomboy
There is no boulder she won't climb
The highest slide she dares to use
At first her fear says "Oh I'm afraid of that ride"
but she goes anyway
First words as she steps off, "Can we do it again?"
Jeans are her favorite clothes
Roughhouse with our dog, and see how wild they can get
She will take on any boy and blame him if trouble begins
But when the day is done and she is played out, she becomes our little girl, and the tomboy will disappear until tomorrow

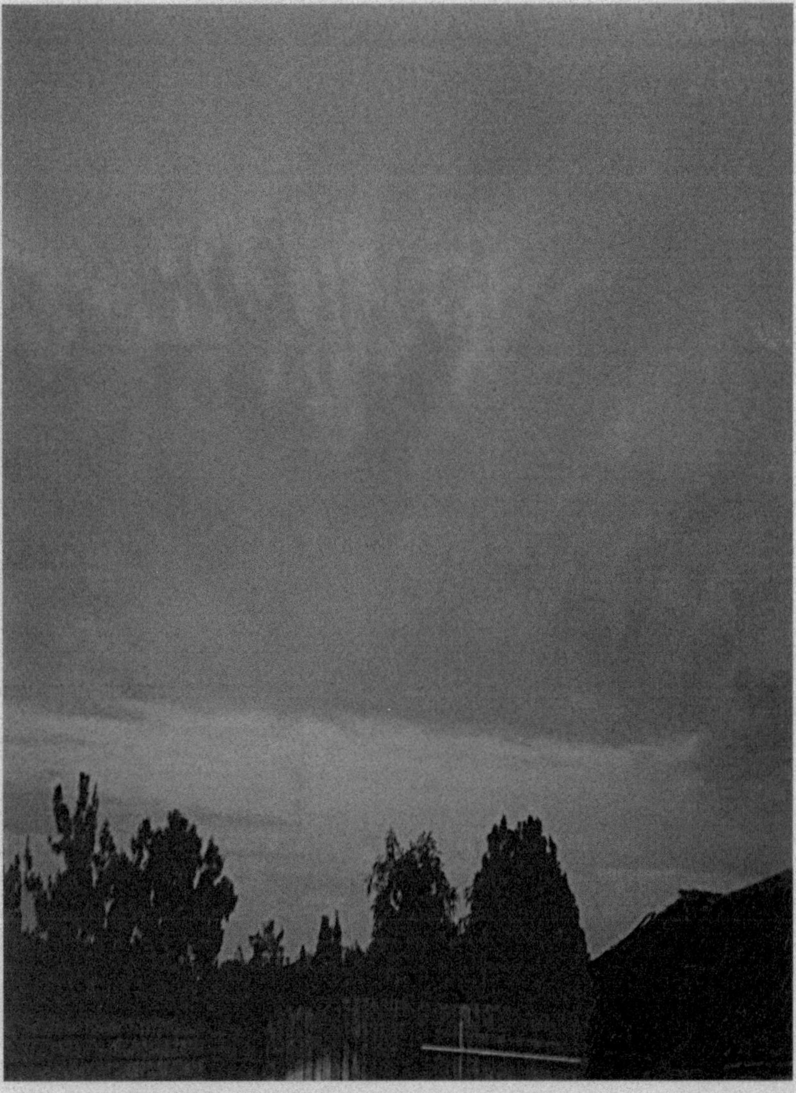

FLAMING SKY

FLAMING SKY

The day is slowly giving up its luster to the darkening skies
Huge towering clouds, bases tinged with ebbing sunlight, form halos of light and dark around the sun
Flames burst forth setting the cloud covered heavens on fire
The wind spreads the boiling masses from east to west
The heaven is turned into fire and ice drifting toward the horizon, then the sun sets and all is dark

THE FILL-IN

Here I am, the fill-in
Your must know what that is
A crumpled piece of newspaper that you jam in the corner of a box to keep your books or dishes from moving around
The raisins added to a salad because the cook forgot the tomatoes
The recipe Aunt Martha puts in her letter because she doesn't want to send one page of nothing
The lady with the not so perfect voice, who takes the place of the lead singer in a choir
The author is running late, so they ask you to speak for 15 minutes, just to fill-in of course
One club member can't make the cruise, would you like to fill-in for her
The teacher calls, please could you make 20 dozen cookies. Mrs. Smith has come down with the mumps
The fill-ins, without them how could the world exist?

SUNFLOWER PEEPING

SUNFLOWER PEEPING

SUNFLOWER PEEPING

I notice an intruder peeping over my fence
Tall and yellow, its face turns towards me,
towering over all
Green hands, oops I mean leaves, wave to attract
my attention
Thinking the sun has risen in the west, I looked
again
The sunflower gazes down upon me, yellow in the
bright sunlight, a beacon of joy in my life.

AFTER THE WEDDING

White lacy gown dropped in haste
Veil tossed to one side
Reams of crumbled, colored wrapping paper
cover the floor
A riot of puffed-up papers, white, bright gold,
fancy red and silver
The wedding is over, the guests have departed
but the marriage has just begun
Marriage is not like folded neat colored paper
everything in its proper place, but like riots of
rumpled variegated wrapping
Smooth at times but then crumpled at others
Always looking for new tomorrows

CANDLE ICE

CANDLE ICE

Welcome aboard, you are about to be
transported back in time to the ice age
Whiteness surrounds and we move towards the
snow-covered blue white glacier
How can we proceed, our small boat is
surrounded by ice, cold and deadly but with a
beauty of its own
Our boat herds the broken pieces of thick
triangular ice away from us as we continue on our
way
Small icebergs come back together as we pass
Approaching the glacier, the ice is translucent but
with a strength that holds us back
As we surge forward it explodes into long slivers
of ice crystals, sending waves of sound across
the ice fields
In the silent presence of the glacier, each contact
of boat and ice rings out like hundreds of crystal
bells chiming
Flashes of brilliant color reflect off each sliver,
diamonds floating in a bath of clear cold water,
catching every ray of sunlight
Candle Ice, it shines and flickers as a flame
burning in a dark room
It reaches out from the light of day and the dark of
night beckoning for all to see its beauty

A CHILD AT PLAY

child lies upon the carpet, arms and legs flying
the breeze
ball goes rolling by, chased by the cat
ne quick, small arm reaches out sending the cat
nd ball rolling
aughter bubbles up and spills out, startling the
mbling cat
ll he can see is waving arms and legs, a
reature to attack
e crouches, waiting to see this monster that
tole his ball, and wonders where it went

FALL

FALL

Fall is the changing of the guard
The landscape slips from bright pink, reds,
lavenders and white to hues of orange, rust,
bright cerise and bare brown trees
First one leaf then whole branches change color
Soon green grass is covered with layers of yellow
and orange
Winter is on its way, gray, white and black but
autumn will take its time until every leaf has fallen

THE WEB

A sprinkle of rain in the morning hours
Cool refreshing air with light wind blowing
As I walk out onto my patio, raindrops nest on an
eye catching object, strings woven together
What is it doing here?
Go and pull it down, it does not belong
No string is this but a huge web
Rain drops clinging to every woven thread
A masterpiece of wondrous artistry
Behold the creature's lair, strung from fence to
patio cover
Tomorrow, the lacy web of magnificent
proportions will be no more
It is just for today, Mr. Spider

STORM

STORM

Fast moving clouds, darkness coming on
The roll of thunder in the distance
Trees start to sway, lightning in the far sky
Daylight into night with the swiftness of a moment
Hide, birds, cover your heads with your wings
Small creatures, find your burrows
Noise upon the roof, plink, plink and then a rush
of rain, water running in the streets, people run
through the drops, children splash in the puddles
Clouds deposit their bounty upon the earth
Wind blowing hard rushes clouds across the sky
Louder grows the thunder, closer the lightning
comes
Then silence, the sun peaks through the rushing
clouds
The air smells fresh and the leaves are shiny
bright
God has cleansed his earth and fed the flowers,
grass, crops, and us
His bounty is overwhelming

CHAPEL

The outdoor chapel nestles in a circle of
magnificent trees
The wind gently blows the newly formed leaves,
dropping empty pods upon the congregation
One huge tree, with roots growing in different
directions, entwines itself forming a giant cross
Its branches form a canopy covering this peaceful
place
The stream, just below the trees, rushes over
pebbles and rocks creating heavenly chimes
The solace of running water cleanses the mind
and body.
God's spirit dwells in this piece of our world
I can feel Him here
His touch is as gentle as the whispering winds

WILDERNESS

WILDERNESS

We leave the Juneau dock and head to Skagway
Leaning against the boat rail, cold from the frigid
wind, we feel the isolation slowly surrounding us
Moving across rough waters we pass islands of
nesting bald eagles
Humpback whales cross our bow and a pod of
killer whales, with newborn calves glowing yellow,
surface on the dark green waters of the bay
So close you could almost touch them
Sea lions use a buoy as a resting area, barking at
us as if to say, this is their water move away
Caribou graze along the big island's shore
The wilderness envelopes us and we become
one with it

FLAMING CANDLES

Flame and heat lick away at the sturdy white
candles
Large craters filled with wax making pools of lava
The candles erupt spilling their hot, white mass
onto the rocks below, then continue to run over
the edge, hardening into lacy fringes
Soon the flames will dies, light will be diminished
and solid form will return

WINTER SILENCE

WINTER SILENCE

From high on the mountains, trees march down to
the lake's frozen edge
Winter snow has covered the hillside and silence
creates a boundary
Low clouds touch the mountains and valleys
below making them one
Majestic trees, their limbs laden with heavy snow,
stand as sentries
Branches form a canopy over bare earth, shelter
for the wild beasts
A breeze ruffles the tree tops and snow falls
disturbing the snow-covered landscape
But silence still prevails from mountain top to
distant valley

REMEMBRANCE

REMEMBRANCE

In a forgotten corner of the potting shed the
flower of remembrance grows
Lush purple blooms extend themselves from
hardy green vines
Not satisfied to stay in one place, they entwine
themselves over all that is there
Sunlight filters through the wide slats warming the
regal, purple blossoms
The flowers reach skyward drinking in the rays of
sun, nectar from the heavens
Wild violets, the royal flower of remembrance

Etching “Gamrie” by James McBey